Tiny Mc

Jenny Beattie

Tiny Moments © 2022 Jenny Beattie

All rights reserved.

No part of this publication may be reproduced, stored in a retrieval system, or transmitted, in any form or by any means, electronic, mechanical, photocopying, recording or otherwise, without the prior written permission of the presenters.

Jenny Beattie asserts the moral right to be identified as author of this work.

Presentation by *BookLeaf Publishing*

Web: www.bookleafpub.com

E-mail: info@bookleafpub.com

ISBN: 9789357690249

First edition 2022

For Tom, Dexter & Beatrix

ACKNOWLEDGEMENT

I'd like to thank Tom, Dexter & Beatrix for sharing the tiny moments, and the big.

To all my family and friends who have ever encouraged me with anything creative - thank you.

Original cover artwork by Beatrix Beattie.

Me

I am Jenny,
which means fair one
and God has been gracious.

It means merciful in Hebrew.
In Celtic it means I am lady of the people.
It means white wave in Greek.
In Cornish, fair and yielding.

In the Urban Dictionary Jenny means
sweet and kind but,
whatever you do,
don't get on my bad side,
apparently.

I know how I like my tea.
I know what you are thinking.
I know how to be forgiving of everything, every second.
And patient.
Don't forget patient.

I know how to control a crowd.
I know how to surf.
I know how to sail and pilot and soar like a bird.

I know how to enter society with my hems let down
because I've done it once already,
in a previous life.

I know when a volcano is about to erupt
and I know how to stop it.
I am a volcano
usually on a Thursday.

I know how the boiler works.
I know how to warm a house, a home.

I am Jenny
which means, fair one.

Washing the Wall

I washed a wall today.

I nudged my coat and there behind it
Was a smudge of winter grey.

Poison.

I moved my coat to the left.
Then removed it entirely from my peg.
And then a scarf. And another coat.
And another.
I stripped the rack of its warmth. All of it gone.

There wasn't just a smudge of winter grey.
The black winter had devoured the wall entirely.
Had crept and inched and swept its way along
Towards the heart of the house,
Hidden beneath the very things
Which had promised to keep the cold and damp out.

I washed a wall today.

When it was clean I opened the front
and let the winter sun
Breathe on it.

Rain

For the first time in a long time
I stopped by the back door and
Stood still and faced outwards and watched the rain
From the inside.

At first I couldn't see it,
Couldn't tune in.
I had to concentrate really hard
Tune out the noises of the inside
And listen for the moisture on the outside.
Squint my eyes and focus on the tall, dark trees
At the very back
Like an optical illusion.

And then the rain hit me.
Drenching my view of the outside
From the inside.
I could see it.

I could see it wherever I switched my gaze.
The dull, wet greys of the patio.
The blades of grass.
The roof of the shed.

Even in the silver sky itself.
What a show.

For the first time in a long time
I stopped by the back door and
Stood still and faced outwards and watched the rain
From the inside.

Moss

I send you the tiny moss garden I found
On an ancient brick wall
On a solitary walk.

I have never seen nature so perfectly formed
And yet miniscule.
Minute moss.
I spent longer than a minute there.

I send you the limes and apples and seaweeds of the
Miniature moss.
Bright against the ancient brick wall.

I would like to spend forever in that moss garden.
To sit,
Read a book and
Lose myself.

Kale

The horizontal sun glanced off my newly dug bed.
I'm no Heaney but,
All the same,
I was proud of my efforts.

I crouched, mud-tinged, and slowly turned towards
The old bed.
The thick mulch eiderdown smothered
The roots and the bare-bottomed stems of the
Sturdy kale.

By god,
Haven't you grown since the last time I saw you?

Year of Jigsaws and Wires

The wires arrived and did not leave.

Wireless was not enough.
Could not be enough
For everything we needed it to be.
We became Wiremore.

The coiled electronics arrived in each separate room.
One at a time.
Then they entered two by two.
Our ark was ready for the
Technological flood.

Soon they passed from room to room
Taped to the floor
Threaded around the door frame and between hinges and
Over corners.
A more permanent fixture.

They connected a boss,
A team,
Colleagues,
A classroom,
Another classroom,
Friends,

A choir with songs in their heart,
A family,
An allotment committee.
A chance to escape their own room into
Someone else's.

There were not enough wires for me.
Or were there too many?
I can't be sure.

I opened the jigsaw
And sought out the four corner pieces.

The Hallway

A woman, heavy with the day,
Comes home.

She takes off her coat
And puts down her bag and throws down her gloves
And kicks off her shoes
And puts them all down in the hallway.

She puts down the cancelled train and the four
half-drunk cups of tea.
The rain that soaked her, she puts that down.
She puts down the headache and the pre-meeting nerves.
The too-hot office and the too-cold meeting-room; they
are put down too.
She puts down the call to her father.
She puts down the banana bread recipe.
She puts down the negative pregnancy test result.
She puts down their disapproval.

The sun streams into the hallway
Through the still open door.
Quickly, she closes it to trap the sunlight there too.
It stays!

Let us go then, you and I
The Love Song of J. Alfred Prufrock is put in the hallway.
Pride of place.
Pride and Prejudice.
Hope. Dreams. Love. Promise.
Him. He gets put in the hallway.

She looks around and sighs.
There is a lot of stuff in her hallway.
It looks cluttered, uncomfortable, bloated.
She clambers over the piles, nearly toppling the mortgage, Alton Towers and paint swatches.
There's a space.
She deftly deposits a card to her Grandpa and her overdue dentist's appointment.
Done.

She utters her thanks to the hallway as she reaches the end of it.
She has carefully woven a pathway from the front door
Through all her stuff in the hallway.
She will need this space later
When she takes the bins out.

How Was My Day?

How was my day?
I typed it away
One finger tap at a time.

The email I sent his teacher.
The WhatsApp I sent my friend.
The text I sent my mum.
The booking I made for that class.
The text reply I sent back to my mum.
The tweet I sent that author.
The update I added to Facebook.
The photograph of the new shoots appearing in my garden with a witty caption to Instagram.
The email to my head of department.
The email to my line manager.
The email to her school.
The email.
The email.
The email.
The email.

How was my day?
I typed it away.
One finger tap at a time.

Gravy

Friday,
I'm going to eat you up.

I'm going to add a generous dollop
Of Greek yogurt with honey,
Chia seeds, flaxseeds, cacao nibs
And a handful of
Blueberries and Raspberries.

I'm going to butter you, thickly.
Add cheese, tomato, rocket
Maybe some spring onions and mayonnaise.
I'm going to slice you into triangles
And have, on the side,
A packet of crisps.

I will shave a modest sliver of you
Making sure to get buttercream
And at least two of the chocolate curls from the top
And serve you on the cake plate with the cake fork that
Grandma bought me for my eighteenth birthday.
I shall fill up the pot with you and
Drink you from a
Cup and saucer.

I shall bury you under
Carrots, cauliflower, cabbage
Broccoli and beans, green of course.
You won't be visible under the mountain of
Roast potatoes.

And, Friday?

I shall drown you in gravy.

Someone Get That

Have you heard her?
She's on the telephone
To the 1980s.

She talking to Top of the Pops
And asking after penny sweets from the local shops.
She-Ra has had trouble with her Walkman but
Michael Knight and Kit are getting a dab hand with the
Rubik's Cube, apparently.

Have you heard her?
She's on the telephone
To the 1980s.

She's dialling up Cabbage Patch Dolls
And asking after the hand knitted leg warmers.
You'll never guess what!
Michael J Fox stuffed Garfield into his car ashtray
all because he wasn't allowed to play his Smash Hits
album in the stereo in the glass cabinet
That he wasn't allowed to touch.

Have you heard her?
She's on the telephone
To the 1980s.

She's returning ET's call now that he's back at home.
See you later, alligator.
In a while Crocodile Dundee.
Oh, those Gremlins on the line
So much crackling.

Have you heard her?
She's on the telephone
To the 1980s

Now I can hear laughing with the fluorescent
Pinks and greens
And Velvet Scrunchie is trying to get in on the call.
But Crimped Hair is dominating.
Transformers are also reminiscing about their heyday
They are old now.
Dallas and Dynasty have still got the big hair and the
Big shoulders
But their skin is a little more wrinkled.

Have you heard her?
She's on the telephone
To the 1980s.

Who you gonna call?

Broken Time

I'm so clumsy.
I appear to have broken time.

I dropped a year on the cold, hard tiles
Of the kitchen floor.
It slipped through my sanitised fingers.
I should have kept hold of it,
Tried to catch it before it hit the ground
But there was nothing I could do.

I gasped
As the year shattered instantly
The months spread out and
The weeks rolled under the kitchen unit.
Days splattered up the walls.
Minutes filled the floor like
A tidal wave of Lego pieces emptied from the tub.
Shards of seconds splintered the air.

What a mess.

I tried to grasp them.
Scoop up the broken time and put it back together again.
I grabbed handfuls but the fragmentsflooded
Between my fingers.

Down, down, down.

I grabbed my dustpan and brush, and a clean cloth, and the broom
And my new cordless handheld hoover that
Delivery Dave
Brought me one lockdown day last May.

I grabbed my dustpan and brush, and a clean cloth, and the broom
And my new cordless handheld hoover
And cleaned away that broken year.
I swept and gathered and sponged and
Wrapped up it up in a huge
Black hole of a bin bag
Tied neatly with a yellow bow.

I must be more careful with time, next time.
Such a waste, to have broken a year like that.

I'm so clumsy.
I appear to have broken time.

But…wait!
I just found an hour stuck to the bottom of my cat's paw.
I'll have to look carefully.
There may be more around and
I would like that.

So

Today a poem just sort of fell out of me...
I don't know how it happened.
I'm normally so careful, so guarded.
I immediately felt guilty of course

Oh, the extravagance!

What will people say? Think?
When they ask me that evening
What did you do today?
And I respond, apologetically,
Oh, a poem just sort of fell out of me...

Oh dear, some will say, *I am sorry to hear that.*
I hope you feel better soon.
I'll pray for you.
My deepest sympathies.

But, with an eye-twinkle and an arm-squeeze
One will whisper,
As she helps me scoop it up:
You lucky thing.
If only I could be that lucky.

Eye-Level

She is at eye level
When I am seated
And she is standing

She has grown

I do not like it

Soon I will be the shortest in the family
And then I shall only see the
Underneath of chins
And armpits
And up nostrils.

I shall never see the top of her head again
And kiss her hair

Unless

She is sitting down
And I am standing.

Rage, My Etna

You rage and burn.
Your words demolish this home.
Your bare foot provokes the wall,
Daring it to make contact.
Luckily for your little toe, the wall refuses.

You turn to me and
I, too, am wounded.
Your fiery words spit out
And hit me straight in my heart.

Breathe.
Both of us need to breathe but
Only one of us can.

Your lava tongue erupts, again.
Your body betrays your sharp voice
And its flailing shows something else.

You are uncomfortable in your skin,
Your growing skin.
The effort of your heavy words
Leaves you exhausted.
You, too, are hurting.

Your furnace dissolves in a hiss.
Your tears have extinguished them.
Flames, tears, words, snot, wasted hours
We are all spent.

I wipe your flames, tears, words, snot, wasted hours away.
I collect everything I can from you.
Unload it onto me.
It is hard to bear on some days.
But I will. And I do.

When I tuck you into bed and
Kiss you goodnight later
I shall whisper,
Sweet dreams, Etna.

And you will mumble back to me
I love you, mum.

And, when I am alone,
And I am certain you are asleep and cannot hear me or
See me cry,
I shall carefully
Unpick every fiery splinter from my heart.
Make a small pile
And put them in the bin.

Shade

There hasn't been much light this
Shady week.
We're tiptoeing on eggshells
Alert to the one careless word which could tip
Everyone over.
Push us all off the edge.
We dance round the house and each other
Careful of toes, looks, hearts.
Everything bruises easily these days.

No, there hasn't been much light this shady week.

I heaved the bins out tonight and looked up.
I could not see the moon.

Last Year's Me

Last night I ran into last year's me.
I nearly collided with her as she scurried from the house
Closing the front door behind her
As quietly as she dared so as not to disturb the children.
She was running slightly late.
I remember that; having a time and a place to be.

I thought to stop her, and tell her:
That she wouldn't get to visit her Grandad next week like she planned,
And the cup of tea and ginger nuts she'd enjoyed with her Nan
Would be the last for a long, long time.

I nearly called out to her as she sped past:
You'll need patience and organisation
And a new alarm time for those trolley queues.
You'll make friends with the local corner shop.
Tomorrow, a neighbour you have never spoken to, will put a note through your door.

I should have warned her:
You'll forget which side the petrol goes into.
You rarely drive now.

You'll realise how much you miss people.
Talking to them. Hugging them.
And you worry about how you'll feel when you get told you can see them again.
Talk to them. Hug them.

I wanted to shake her:
You'll have to learn anew and unlearn so many old habits, hopes, loves.
Your children will need feeding, constantly.
You will find it hard to pick up a book.
You won't learn a new language or a new instrument
You will have strange, vivid dreams which leave you completely spent every morning,
Completely unready for the next Groundhog Day.

Instead, I let her walk away from me
And envied her healthy pre-lockdown length hair and slightly less full figure.
She turned unexpectedly, caught my eye and half-smiled.
I nodded my head in her direction,
Willing her to enjoy her last night
Before the world changed.
I remember that: having a time and a place to be.
I still do.
It's just different now.

Four Tickets to Ryde

We are waiting for the Isle of Wight to reopen
We are waiting for the staff to
Open the shutters on Cowes
Turn off the Sandown alarm.
Let some air in through the Bembridge windows.
Turn on the Seaview tills
Restyle the Newport mannequins.

We want to walk down the aisles of Shanklin
And fill our baskets with Ventnor and Brighstone and Yarmouth.

We want to see for ourselves the latest Ryde
And feel the softness of its fabric
And how the cut of it flatters the hip
And how the hemline sits perfectly
And whether the label is scratchy.

We are waiting for the Isle of Wight to reopen
Let's dig out the credit card buried in the sand and
Go and sit in a deckchair.

Catch

I don't remember
How nervous I was driving to your house
That first time, that first Christmas.

Or how I smoothed down my clothes and ironed
The creases of my brow.
Respectable.
A good impression.

Or how long the presents had taken to wrap
Carefully thought, carefully bought
Carefully brought.

I don't remember any of that.

Instead, I remember your smile
As you opened the oak-heavy door.
How you grabbed my bags, my gifts
How you grabbed my heart
And I flew away.

I remember you
Dancing your head under low-flying beams
To stand up straight beside me
Clasping my hand

Pulling me towards you.
Towards your parents.

I tripped. Stumbled.

Catch.

I remember you, all of you
From the first.

I fell and you caught me.
You catch me every single day.

9.30am On a Friday Morning

Let me meet you at the coffee shop on the high street at 9.30am
On a Friday morning, our day off.

Let me be early and hold the door open for
An elderly couple who smile at me with
False white teeth
And a group of friends loaded with
Lattes and muffins.

Let me scoop up an adventurous toddler
Who crashed into my legs
While watching the bus on the road
And hand them back to their smiling grown up
Who gives my arm a squeeze in thanks.

Let me see you walking down the street towards me
And then we both begin to run in slow motion
Like they do in the films.

Let us wrap our arms around each other
Our coats, our bags, our months without, our hearts
And let us squeal as we rock side to side
Still hugging.

Let us link arms and
Enter the coffee shop on the high street at 9.31am
On a Friday morning, our day off.

Let us order a *tea with milk*
And a *skinny blueberry muffin*
And a *coffee I can never remember the name of,*
Yes please, with *chocolate on the top*,
And *an almond croissant*, the king of croissants,
And *two tap waters*.
Yes, all on the same tray will be fine.
Thank you.

Let us sink into the sofa,
Both on the same sofa
With two empty chairs facing us.

Let us talk and crash arms and knock knees and
My, look at your nails and look at my hair
And I'm sorry you're feeling that way
And it's been so long and I can't believe it
And, is anything bringing you joy?

You're real and I've missed you

Let me meet you at the coffee shop on the high street at 9.30am
Every Friday morning, our day off.

We've missed a lot.

Sunshine Sonata

We walk, hand in hand, the three of us.
I'm in the middle, keeping the peace.
Short shadows dance just in front of us.

The relentless rain ceased a fortnight ago.
The snow and ice briefly brightened our landscape with
Something solid to slide on.
The mud has now dried and our trainers kick up
Clouds of dust.
Wellington boots would be a step too far today.

It is the last day of winter
The chilled sun blazes our faces
As we tentatively undo the zip on our
Winter coat.

They talk and talk and talk.

Stop.

We stand still in the middle of the path.
I ask them to *close your eye*s.
They both giggle but do as I say.

I see a moment pass across their faces.

Listen.

We listen for the silence.
Their faces quieten as they turn them a fraction higher
Towards the sun.
We listen for the silence
But it is lost.

With eyes closed and the February sun
Burning away our worries
We listen
And hear nothing but birdsong.
A thousand million songs filling the February sky
which a moment ago had been drowned out by
Two bickering bundles.

After an unusual minute or two
I tug gently on their hands.
Their eyes flutter open as our feet begin marking the
Dusty path once again.

He is off, kicking his football half a pitch away.

She edges closer, confidingly.
I liked that.

The Laughter is Loud

The laughter is loud
And finally allowed in the garden.
It is blooming.

They roar all day long.
It is wonderful to hear
After being in such a silent landscape
For so long.

I cannot hear the birds.
For the first time in ages
Their fragile song is shattered
By the amplified voices
Each clamouring to be heard,
Seen in the sunshine
Like a tall sunflower.

The laughter is loud
And finally allowed in the garden.
It is blooming.
Music to my ears.

Milton Keynes UK
Ingram Content Group UK Ltd.
UKHW020655200923
429044UK00015B/463